My Elephant, My Friend

Written by Vanessa York
Photography by Ted Wood

India

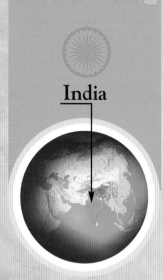

Bomman lives in a village in the Nilgiri Hills, in southern India. His father is an elephant handler. Bomman is learning how to take responsibility for an elephant, too. Today, there are not many jobs for elephant handlers, so Bomman must become very good at handling and caring for his elephant to get the job he wants.

responsibility being trusted with something

Contents

My Elephant, My Friend

My name is Bomman, and my best friend is an elephant called Mudumalai (*MUD uh muh lie*). My father is a mahout. I am learning to be a mahout, too. Mahouts are highly respected in India, but today, there are not many jobs for them.

In the old days, logging was the main job. Now, logging is not allowed in the forests near my home. Mahouts and their elephants now take care of the forest and the wildlife.

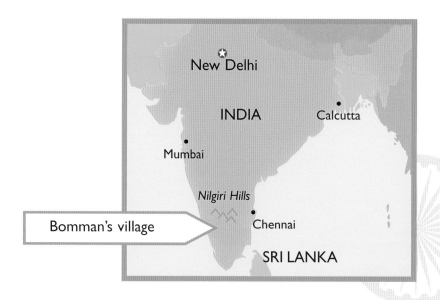

New Delhi

INDIA   Calcutta

Mumbai

Nilgiri Hills

Bomman's village   Chennai

SRI LANKA

mahout   a person who rides and trains elephants

In our village, an elephant stands beside nearly every house.

Every morning, I ride Mudumalai down to the river to give him a bath. Climbing onto my friend's back can be hard, but he helps me. He holds out his front leg, and I climb it like a ladder.

Mudumalai lowers himself into the water.
Then my father and I scrub him from trunk
to tail. Elephants are ticklish, so we scrub hard.

Mudumalai likes being washed. He rolls onto his side and waves his trunk. He sprays water into the air.

What kinds of jobs do you share with your parents?

Then we take Mudumalai into
the forest. I ride and my father walks,
so he can watch and train me.

I tell Mudumalai what to do with my voice
or my feet. I can use words like "Go," "Back up,"
"Push," and "Pull." If I rub my feet up behind
his ears, he knows it means "Stand up."
Rubbing my feet down his ears means "Sit."

Mahouts Today

Long ago, elephants were used for logging and transport. Now these jobs are usually done by trucks and machines. Today, there are more than 33,000 elephants in India, and more than 5,000 of them are trained. Trained elephants help control wild elephants in the forest and keep them away from farms and crops.

Elephants are also used in cities. They are used in festivals and in ceremonies at many temples. In the city, even elephants must obey the traffic laws!

ceremony   an organized event to mark a special occasion

11

Mudumalai eats bamboo. We cut bamboo in the forest. Mudumalai carries the huge pile back to the village with his trunk and tusks. He will eat all of it in about two days.

Caring for an elephant is a big responsibility, but I am proud to call my elephant my friend.

bamboo   a plant with strong, hollow stems

Explore India

India is a very big country in southern Asia. More people live in India than in any other country except China.

India's landscape is full of contrasts. There are great rivers, mountains, plains, deserts, and tropical rain forests.

India has a large technology industry. These children are learning how to use a computer.

The capital city of India is New Delhi. It was carefully planned when it was built in the early 1900s. New Delhi replaced Delhi as India's capital in 1931. The cities are just 3 miles apart.

On the Go!

Where would you find Bollywood?
Go to page 17

What is dal?
Go to page 20

Who is Ganesh?
Go to page 23

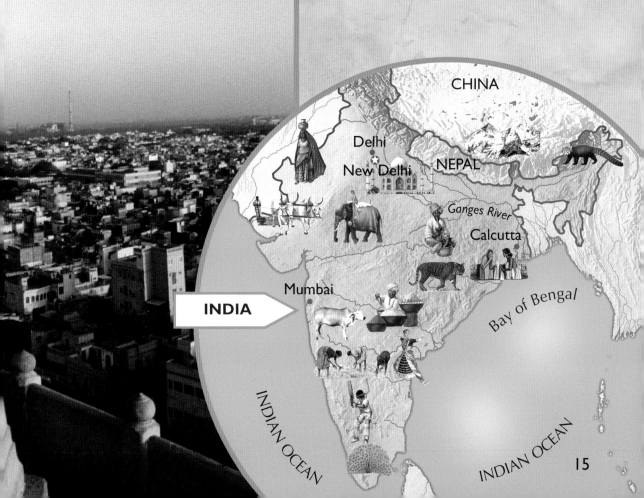

CHINA

Delhi

New Delhi

NEPAL

Ganges River

Calcutta

INDIA

Mumbai

Bay of Bengal

INDIAN OCEAN

INDIAN OCEAN

Town and Country

Most people in India live in villages and work in the fields. They grow crops for the markets. Many Indian people spend their whole lives in their home village without ever moving to another place.

Many people also live in large, crowded cities and towns. Beautiful temples and buildings can be found all over India.

The city of Mumbai is by the Indian Ocean. Hundreds of years ago, it was a fishing village. Now it is the largest city in India.

Did You Know?

"Bollywood" is the name given to India's huge, popular film industry based in Mumbai. The name comes from combining *Bombay* (the former name of Mumbai) with *Hollywood*, the famous center of the U.S. film industry.

Almost all Bollywood films have a handsome hero and a beautiful heroine. They are filled with singing, dancing, comedy, and exciting stunts.

Brightly colored posters advertise Bollywood movies.

Ways of Life

India is so large that each region has different types of food and different styles of clothing. However, in every part of India, families are very important. Many people share their homes with extended families.

No matter what part of India they are from, many Indian women wear brightly colored saris.

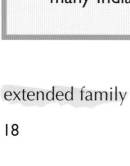

extended family   a family living together that can include grandparents, aunts, uncles, and cousins

Cricket is the most popular sport in India.

A family enjoys a picnic beside one of India's many temples.

How many people are there in your extended family?

Spice It Up

Curry is a mixture of hot and flavorful spices. It is used in many Indian foods. Rice, dal, and vegetables are eaten at most meals, and meat or fish curries are enjoyed about once a week. Bread is also part of most meals.

Indian food has become popular in restaurants throughout the world.

dal a dish made of spicy lentils, beans, or peas

A type of flat bread, called roti, is baked in a special oven and sold on the street.

Many Indian people enjoy spicy snack food. Snack sellers make and sell snacks on the streets. The smell of spices fills the air.

Celebrations

There are many festivals in India. Holi is a festival that marks the end of winter. To celebrate, people throw colored water and powders at each other. There are dances and parades. Diwali is called the Festival of Lights. People line up lamps on their roofs and outside their houses. There are fireworks and feasts.

Elephants are an important part of many celebrations.

A dancer celebrates Holi.

Did You Know?

The Hindu god Ganesh has an elephant's head. Ganesh is the god of food. Children like his festival because on that day they are allowed to eat lots of their favorite sweets!

What Do You Think?

1 How is life in Bomman's village the same as where you live? How is it different?

2 What skills do you think Bomman would need to be a good mahout?

How does Bomman show responsibility for Mudumalai?

Index